# HILLARIOUS

# HILLARIOUS

The Wacky
Wit, Wisdom, and Wonderment
of Hillary Rodham-Clinton

George Grant

Adroit Press
Franklin, Tennessee

Unless otherwise noted, all Scripture quotations are either the
author's own translations or are from the New King James
Version of the Bible, © 1984 by Thomas Nelson, Inc.,
Nashville, Tennessee.

ISBN: 0–9633469–0–3

Adroit Press
P.O. Box 680365
Franklin, Tennessee 37068

To Karen and Debbie
Who Share a Genuine
Wit, Wisdom, and Wonderment
That Is Anything But Wacky

*Deus Vult*

# CONTENTS

# *APOLOGIA*

*He who sits in the heavens shall laugh;
He shall hold them in derision. Then He
shall speak to them in His wrath, and
distress them in His deep displeasure.*

*Psalm 2:4–5*

I t is crucial that we be able to find humor in the doings of the modern world," the great wag G. K. Chesterton once remarked. "It is a profound testament to our confidence in providence that we be able to acknowledge the sheer absurdity in the things of fallen creation. This is not a spirit of meanness, rather it is a sober-minded recognition that if a thing is not right, it is silly as well as wicked . . . this is our apologia, not our apology."[1] I must confess that I never fully understood what he meant by that remarkable epistemological quip until I experienced the wild ride of this project. Thankfully, I had a number of kind-hearted souls who helped me see the lighter side of these dark and dire days—and thus made the book possible.

Several friends—old and new—scoured the countryside to help me gather the necessary research and pull together the necessary resources. Mary Jane Morris, Jerry and Linda Bowyer, Bruce Tippery, Bob Pambianco, Michael Skaggs, John Gissy, and Clark Eberly selflessly combed the files, manned the phones, loaded the faxes, scanned the microfiche, and ran the copiers—all *gratis* and all at a furious pace. Stacy and Coby Owens dropped everything and performed yeoman's duty for me by excavating sundry arcane and esoteric absurdia on a moment's notice. The staffs of the Vanderbilt University library, Washington Times, C-Span Cable Network, *Human Events*, the *American Spectator*, the Capital Research Center, *Insight*, *World*, and the Conservative Caucus were extremely helpful as well. To all these, I am deeply grateful.

R. Emmett Tyrrell, Jr., P. J. O'Rourke, Taki, and Rush Limbaugh helped to clarify my thinking, sharpen my tongue, and improve my vocabulary.

Special thanks go to Tom Singleton, Jamie O'Rourke, and Bill Taylor for their belief in—and support of—this project. Their faithful stewardship is a constant encouragement to me.

As always my publisher, David Dunham, was the quintessential literary coach—an unrelenting taskmaster and a beloved friend all rolled into one. One of these days he is going to let me write a book at a nice leisurely pace—he promised.

The soundtrack was provided by Susan Ashton, Out of the Grey, Kemper Crabb, and Charlie Peacock, and the midnight musings were supplied by J. I. Packer, Ellis Peters, and Hillaire Belloc.

My wife, Karen, was unswerving in her support for me during the furious days and nights of traveling, writing, compiling, and editing. All that I do and all that I am relies entirely upon her strength and resolve.

The wildness of this world lies in wait for the unsuspecting. But in God's good providence, that wildness has been at least partially tamed for me by these: my friends, loved ones, and fellow-laborers.

Wandrille Fest, 1992
New York

## Part One

# HYPE

*The wise in heart will receive commands, but a prating fool will fall. He who walks with integrity walks securely, but he who perverts his ways will become known. He who winks with the eye causes trouble, but a babbler will fall.*

*Proverbs 10:8–10*

According to Al Gore—Slick Willie's young-gun veepster—the 1992 election is "about a lot more than politics, sound-bites, or photo-ops."[1] For once in his life, he's right. That is precisely why we should look past all the campaign hoopla to his Party's behind-closed-doors substantive core.

We should thus forget about all that we have seen in the gratuitously sympathetic liberal media—from the carefully-scripted high-tech show that Ron Brown, Linda Bloodworth-Thomason, and Ann Richards staged for prime-time viewers during July, to the whistle-stop retro-marketing stunts that the candidates staged through the early days of the magical-mystery-tour campaign. The real story of the Democratic Party lies beyond the pall of the handlers. It lies beyond the red, white, and blue multi-media antics within Madison Square Garden or before the fawning and yammering of press legions. It lies beyond the small-town Mom and apple pie images projected onto arena video-walls or bunted along the perimeter of midwestern Amtrak or Greyhound stations.

At the Democratic National Convention, just out of sight of the cloying cultural-contras at the official delegation fetes and feasts, the essence of

Democratic politics made itself all too evident. Gathered together in one place from every nook and cranny from coast to coast, they spread their deleterious effects and showed their true colors.

And I can assure you, it was not a pretty sight.

## The Garden Party

An old Chinese proverb intones: "Walk a mile in your adversary's sandals and you will better understand his cares." Now to be sure, I'm not much on eyeing fortune cookie logic or toeing Birkenstock comfort, but in a moment of weakness I did think that it would be interesting to mix and mingle with the faithful during the convention festivities in New York City. I wanted to go incognito of course, but that proved to be more than a little difficult—since I have a fairly nondescript haircut and wear fairly nondescript clothes and behave in a fairly nondescript fashion in public. Even so, I tried to blend in as best I could—given those inherent difficulties.

Despite all the emphasis during the stump-thumping, prime-time platform speeches on "putting people first, revitalizing the American dream, and stimulating the flagging economy,"[2] the most telling activities at the convention—as one might well have expected—revolved around the concerns of the tried and true Party activists: the homosexual health-care extortionists and the feminist, child-killing enthusiasts.

The sundry street-savvy shock-troops of Act Up and Queer Nation—along with members of the newest and most radical AIDS faction who apparently call themselves Moby's Dick—planned several lively events for the convention, including a "kiss-in," a "condom-fest," and an "in-your-face rally" in Central Park. Call me an old-fogey, or a dwem-bore, or a party-pooper, but I simply couldn't bring myself to attend any of them. I'm just not the adventurous sort. Besides, I have a weak stomach.

Thus, I was forced to confine my infiltration fling to the abortion battlements of the feminazi, sensitivity-or-else crowd.

Aside from a few carefully planned and orchestrated "spontaneous" demonstrations, the *big* convention-week event for these haute-assassins was a "march for choice" through midtown Manhattan and around Madison Square Garden where the Post-Perot Sex-and-Gore ticket was frantically putting on its states-man-like happy face for a proliferation of doting media-dinks. I took a deep breath and decided to tag along.

The humidity was high, the temperature was higher, and the passions were higher still as marchers gathered at the rally site. At first there seemed to be more New York police than demonstrators, but before long the crowd swelled to about three thousand—not bad for a metropolitan area that boasts some thirty million inhabitants.

It was a predictably shabby lot. In fact, it looked to be the sort of hippyish rent-a-crowd that tends to populate odious Earth Day celebrations, moribund Oliver Stone movies, and antediluvian Grateful Dead concerts. The only individuals I thought I recognized were Ellie Smeal—who flashed her trademark Wild-Woman-of-Borneo grin—and Whoopie Goldberg—who was wearing what I took to be some sort of African tribal costume designed to complement her dreadfully matted dreadlock hairdo. Though I admit that first impressions are frightfully unreliable—not at all unlike weathermen, Ramblers, and public opinion polls—it seemed to me that just about everyone else looked like they had just emerged from a jungle, too—or at the very least from a zoo. I even heard a few of them growling and roaring in anxious anticipation of their twenty-block urban prowl.

The organizer of the demonstration—an emaciated sixties wanna-be with an angry voice that sounded like a wheezy dust-buster with a Bronx accent—gave everyone their instructions about how and where to march. Besides her

Democratic Party credentials, she was somehow connected with a freshly-minted and hastily-loaded loose cannon called the Women's Action Coalition—its credo is "revolt," its colors are "black and blue," and its *modus operandi* is "high octane anger." The woman standing before me wielded her beat-up bull-horn like a bazooka—and was thus convincing evidence of those so-briquets.

Although the WAC was sponsoring and co-ordinating the march, most of the other radical fringe groups that make up the Democrats' re-markable "Party of Inclusion" were also well represented. Members of Act Up, Queer Nation, and Moby's Dick had taken a break from their respective merry-making to join in. Planned Parenthood officials circulated among the marchers, as did NOW representatives. In fact, the regular litany of liberalism's lallop were all present and accounted for: the ACLU, the Fund for the Feminist Majority, NARAL, People for the American Way, the NEA, Sierra Club, CIS-PES, Greenpeace, and Amnesty International. It was a veritable save-the-starving-third-world-lesbian-codependent-whales family reunion.

The march leader had a hard time constructing a complete coherent sentence, but she spoke with passionate authority nonetheless. Everyone around me was nodding as if they understood her completely—so I pretended that I was in on the gag too. Moments later formations assembled and the whole lot made off ranting and raving into the sweltering afternoon.

Whenever the Boy Scouts or the Marine Corps march, they count cadence with singsong rhymes. Not to be outdone, these bolshieblustering comrades-in-arms along Broadway began to chant:

"Not the church. Not the state. Women must decide their fate."

"Keep your rosaries off my ovaries."

"What do we want? Choice. When do we want it? Always."

"Stop the violence. End the war against women."

"He is crazy. He is scary. And his name is Randall Terry."

"Abortion is health care. Health care is a right."

Those, of course, are only the slogans that can be decently reprinted here. There were plenty of others, I'm sorry to say. In fact, the two girls marching alongside me—it took me a while to confirm that they were indeed girls because their crew cuts, parachute pants, army boots, and tattoos threw me for a moment or two—seemed especially to enjoy the ones that can't be reprinted here. They giggled and nudged one another knowingly whenever some crude anatomical function was mentioned—the sheer profundity of their discourse rather reminded me of the whispered conversations I once strained to overhear in the locker-room following gym class in the sixth-grade.

The signs that the marchers carried, too, were viciously vulgar. Besides the tried and true—like, "Keep abortion legal," "We won't go back," "No more nice girls," and others—a rambunctious group wearing T-shirts emblazoned with "Dykes on Bykes" flaunted placards and posters that would make a sailor blush. I honestly had not seen such profligate profanity since my brief stint as a janitor at a truck stop—back when I was still trying to put myself through graduate school.

As befits any political rally worth its salt, most of the marchers wore a bevy of buttons—the more the merrier. Some lampooned Bush or Quayle, some proselytized for Clinton or Gore, and some pressed home the mundania of the pro-abortion cant. A button that seemed to be very popular was one that fairly demanded, "Hillary's husband for president." Another that seemed to be liberally distributed amongst the partisans read, "Hillary: Come hell or high water." I took it that the bearers of such sentiments meant them—perhaps all too literally.

As the parade passed the corner of 52nd Street, several well-endowed but scantily-clad women emerged from a seedy topless bar called

"Flashdancers." The day before they had bared all for convention-goers in front of Madison Square Garden. Since Teddy Kennedy has recently remarried and Slick Willie has been taken out of circulation—for the time being—by his prudent handlers, I guess they were desperate to drum up new business for their establishment. At any rate, the girls were happily received into line—thus lending new credibility to the Democratic dogma of multi-cultural inclusion and to New York's favorite mondo-moniker, "The Naked City."

Amazingly—to me at least—most of the passers-by along the route through Times Square ignored the marchers altogether. Apparently, they see stranger sights than this just about every day of the week—though for the life of me, I can't fathom how. A few Japanese tourists did look up from their furious shopping sprees long enough to take a few snapshots, but otherwise the three thousand haranguers were lost amidst all the other sights, sounds, and smells of New York—each one eerily unpleasant in its own right.

I had to wonder what the marchers thought of this unexpected oddity. So, I braved querying the two skin-heads to my left:

"Why isn't anyone paying attention to the parade?"

Stupid me. Without answering, they turned a steely stare of utter incredulity my way. At that moment it occurred to me that neither of the girls appeared to be securely anchored by the laws of gravity—in fact, their mental processes seemed already to be hurtling out of earth's orbit.

"Every one is ignoring the march," I tried.

Nothing. Nothing except their twin Uncle Fester glares.

"New York is already pro-choice. So is the Democratic Party. There is no one here to convince. So what is the point?"

At last I saw signs of angry cognition on their faces. Slowly words formed on their lips. In unison they replied: "Hillary."

"Hillary?" I asked.

"Hillary," they answered. "Hillary is the key."

Obviously, the expression on my face begged for a more thorough answer, but that was all that I was to get. Looking back from the vantage of reasoned memory, perhaps I was expecting too much. Perhaps that is all the answer that there is.

Hillary. Hillary is the key.

## The H-Bomb

More often than not, activists either incorrectly convey what they do mean or correctly convey what they do not mean. But, after some reflection, I sensed that these two ardent marchers had somehow stumbled headlong into a central truth—perhaps *the* central truth of the 1992 campaign. Hillary Rodham-Clinton is indeed the key.

In a bizarre election year of twists, turns, and tumults—when just about every other bet is off—this one thing is certain. On it, practically everyone is now agreed.

According to the *Wall Street Journal*:

> To a large degree, the fate of Mr. Clinton's political ambition rests in the hands of his blunt, strong-willed, and critics say, strident wife.[3]

*Newsweek* magazine says:

> Hillary Rodham-Clinton is a driving force in her husband's political career, his best friend and closest adviser, a full partner in Clinton's pursuit of the presidency ... she is the dominant personality in the race ... the only question now is whether she is an asset or a liability.[4]

The *New York Times* agrees:

> She is the dominant figure in the election regardless of how campaign officials may position her. The destiny of the Democratic strategy ultimately lies with her.[5]

*Vanity Fair* intones:

> It is Hillary Rodham-Clinton, lawyer-activ-ist-teacher-author-corporate boardwoman-mother and wife of *Billsomething*, who is the diesel engine powering the front-running Democratic campaign.[6]

And, according to Gail Sheehy, while Bill Clinton may be "the Party's messenger," Hillary is "its message."[7]

Though practically everyone acknowledges that Hillary is indeed likely to be the key to election results come November, not everyone is particularly happy about the situation. Seasoned and pragmatic Democrats believe that her hands-on involvement in the campaign may very well prove to be a prescription for disaster. Privately, many are throwing full-fledged tizzy-fits over Hillary. "Off the record?" confides one. "A f#☆*ing disaster."[8] Another says she is a "nuclear time bomb."[9] Still another calls her "mighty mouth."[10] One has even gone so far as to dub her "Wilhelmina Horton."[11]

The reason is simple. She is the epitome of everything that the left-leaning perennial-losers in the Party have stood for over the past fifty years. She is the perfect incarnation of the radical fringe that has successfully taken over its institutional apparatus. Her petulant big government tax-and-spend socialist antiphon is its archaic call-to-arms. She is its standard-bearer, its champion, and its inspiration. For all the brave talk of shifting the Party's center of gravity, she is clear evidence that it has yet to shed the awful spectre of domineering red-diaper wonks. Thanks to her single-handed efforts, the L-word still properly applies to the Democratic Party—and it applies with a vengeance.

According to Daniel Wattenberg:

> Hillary Clinton has been likened to Eva Peron, but it's a bad analogy. Evita was worshipped by the *shirtless ones*, the working class, while Hillary's charms elude most outside of an elite cohort of left-liberal, baby-boom feminists—the type who thought Anita Hill should be canonized and *Thelma and Louise* was the best movie since *Easy Rider*. Hillary reckons herself the next Eleanor Roosevelt. But, standing well to the left of her husband and enjoying an independent power base within his coalition, Hillary is best thought of as the Winnie Mandela of American politics. She has likened the American family to slavery, thinks kids should be able to sue their parents to resolve family arguments, and during her tenure as a foundation officer gave away millions (much of it in no-strings-attached grants) to the left—including sizable sums to hard-left organizers.[12]

That suits the Carter-Mondale-Dukakis activists just fine. Jim Hightower, for instance, the tub-thumping Texas populist, says Bill Clinton and Al Gore have reputable enough "liberal instincts." But what has enabled Hightower to actively endorse their ticket are the "good people" they have surrounded themselves with, "starting with Hillary."[13] Others have said that while they remain wary of Clinton's regular nods to moderate sensibilities, their fears are quelled by his wife's strong presence in the campaign. As the *Wall Street Journal* reported, "They may wonder about Bill, but they're sure about Hillary. She is the essential glue of his unlikely Democratic coalition."[14]

She is, indeed, quite a piece of work.

Over the years she has endorsed every kooky *outré* cause imaginable, from nationalization of medical care to protected perversion in the arts, from Rousseauian eco-tyranny to child-killing on demand, and from usurpation of parental rights to extending "minority" status to homosexual activists.[15] She has served on the board of the Children's Defense Fund—a radical advocacy group that espouses a comprehensive day-care agenda that would essentially turn the government into a kind of coercive nanny state.[16] She worked for years with the Legal Services Corporation—a federally funded juridical nemesis of constitutional construction.[17] She chaired the New World Foundation—a pet philanthropy for ideological extremists, provincial insurgents, and the few-remaining Marxist-Leninist fellow travelers.[18] She has lent her support to such far-left crackpots as the Christic Institute, the Center for Constitutional Studies, Fairness and Accuracy in Reporting, the Salvadoran communist rebels in CISPES, the National Lawyers Guild, and the Institute for Policy Studies.[19]

In short, she stands four-square on the old failed humanistic agenda of the Democratic Party that has progressively engendered vice, encouraged indolence, crippled the family, invited irresponsibility, perverted justice, inhibited economic progress, and undermined faith throughout this once great land.

Thus, the *National Review* has accurately asserted:

> Hillary Rodham-Clinton's activism threatens her husband's candidacy by linking it to a class of people who are not just indifferent but hostile to Middle America.[20]

People like the angry marchers parading down Seventh Avenue in New York.

## The Real Thing

When I left the marchers, they had just circled Madison Square Garden and were hurling grave insults at anyone and everyone within earshot—particularly if they happened to be men. It occurred to me that such exhibitionistic temper-tantrums are a lot like isometric exercises—they are a real strain, but they don't actually get you anywhere. Thus, despite their ominous and odious appearance, their effect is not so much subversion as silliness.

Their whole movement—from Hillary on down—is a mile wide and an inch deep. They have no real notion of right and wrong—because they have no real notions. They have a clear conscience—despite their awful barbarities—because they have an empty mind. It is a movement built on little more than piffle, drivel, and swill. It is absurd. It is hysterical. It is *hillarious.*

Witness the sundry musings of the most ambitious, the most politically astute, and the most ideologically pure political wife to appear on the world stage since Madame Mao. After reading them, the only question that will remain in your mind should be, "Is Hillary Rodham-Clinton and her political goggle frightening or just funny?"

This collection is offered with the firm conviction that the best case *against* the platform of social transformation and family disintegration that Hillary and her ranting, marching, and blustering cohorts advocate, is precisely their own case *for* it.

Thus, Part Two of this book is just that: an anthology of Hillary's wacky wit, wisdom, and wonderment. It is her wildly whimsical world-view stated in her own words. Hard to believe, I know. But true.

One Clinton campaign adviser has lamented:

> She seems so poised and intelligent and yet she always seems to be one smart remark away from getting in trouble.[21]

Let's just hope he is right.

## Part Two

# HYPERBOLE

*To do evil is like sport to a fool, but a man of understanding has wisdom. The fear of the wicked will come upon him, and the desire of the righteous will be granted. When the whirlwind passes by, the wicked is no more, but the righteous has an everlasting foundation.*

*Proverbs 10:23–25*

## “ I suppose I could have stayed at home and baked cookies and had teas. ”

1992: Hillary offending full-time homemakers while defending herself against a barrage of conflict-of-interest charges in Arkansas politics.[1]

66 **D**ecisions about motherhood and abortion, schooling, cosmetic surgery, treatment of venereal disease, or employment, and others where the decision or lack of one will significantly affect the child's future should not be made unilaterally by parents. 99

1979: Hillary translating the old dog-ate-my-homework justification into modern legal theory: escape the consequences of bad ideas through the simple imposition of brutish state coercion.[2]

## Sixties Jabberwocky

“ **E**very protest, every dissent . . . is unabashedly an attempt to forge an identity in this particular age. That attempt at forging for many of us over the past four years has meant coming to terms with our humanness. ”

1969: Hillary waxing eloquent in the grand intellectual tradition of Alan Alda, Bozo, Sinead O'Connor, Rin Tin Tin, and Geraldo Rivera.[3]

" A letter sent out several years ago about the Child and Family Development Act urged persons to oppose the proposed bill because it would, according to the writers, allow the children to take parents to court if they were ordered to take out the garbage. Family disagreements that result in legal battles are, of course of a more serious nature.

The most recent example of a disagreement between parent and child is found in the abortion cases recently decided by the United States Supreme Court. The Court held that a minor child might seek an abortion without her parents' consent and over her parent's objections if a court believed it to be in the child's best interests. **"**

1979: Hillary assuring jurists that the government would allow for parental discretion in "petty" matters under her proposed child advocacy regulations and thus would usurp their authority only in "important" matters—what a relief that is.[4]

# **I**'m not sitting here, some little woman standing by her man like Tammy Wynette. **""**

1992: Hillary justifying her continuing commitment to her marriage despite widespread rumors of her husband's profligate marital infidelity and sax solos.[5]

## The Only Absolute Is
## That There Are No Absolutes

" **A** rejection of absolutism is welcome. "

1977: Hillary mounting her soap box—government intervention to insure children's rights—to decry the notion that there are certain things that are not altered by the winds of change or the waters of circumstance.[6]

66 **T**here are some things we feel, feelings that our prevailing, acquisitive and competitive corporate life, including tragically the universities, is not the way of life for us. 99

1969: Hillary articulating a worldview as lurid as those toshy novels about self-discovery written by spurned mistresses.[7]

66 **T**here is nothing in my life or work that could be construed as disparaging women who choose to stay home and raise a family. 99

1992: Hillary backpeddling furiously on her earlier tragically hip feminist caricature of stay-at-home wives and mothers.[8]

# "We grew up in a decade dominated by dreams and disillusionment."

1992: Hillary singing the victimization *troparia* and *contakia*—so prolix, so weary, and so otiose of their way—so that you almost want to weep.[9]

<big>**"I**</big>t's a real honor for me to be ever compared to Eleanor Roosevelt. **"**

1992: Hillary confirming the long-suspected connection between the Young Dem's New Covenant and the Old Dem's New Deal—as well as details on who really wears the pants in the Bubba Brigade.[10]

" **P**art of it is a generational thing. Sometimes people in the press are very anxious to come up with categories that explain reality in a way they can grasp. You strip away the complexity of a person to try to grasp at simply enough to be able to talk about it. "

1992: Hillary analyzing with sublime Twelve-Step logic why she believes she has such a high negative rating with the electorate—blaming it on someone else.[11]

## Big Brother Is Helping

"**A**mericans need help understanding their world now more than ever. "

1992: Hillary deriding the vices of television by deriding the viewers of television.[12]

" The basic rationale for depriving people of rights in a dependency relationship is that certain individuals are incapable or undeserving of the right to take care of themselves and consequently need social institutions specifically designed to safeguard their position. Along with the family, past and present, examples of such arrangements include marriage, slavery, and the Indian reservation system. "

1982: Hillary comparing the marriage covenant to the institution of slavery—in the same way that other consensus terrorists yoke together individual liberty and individual perversion, or personal choice and personal brutality.[13]

## The Original Party Animal

" We're searching for more immediate, ecstatic, and penetrating modes of living. "

1969: Hillary shuffling lesser dignities—like life, liberty, and the pursuit of happiness—in order to satisfy the earnest demands of personal peace and affluence.[14]

# " I am not that significant a target on my own. "

1992: Hillary bemoaning the careful scrutiny that a national campaign brings to the brash twogs and niche-marketing nit-wits that rise like slag to the top of the Democratic Party cauldron.[15]

## Something to Look Forward to

**" I** expect to be involved in helping to bring about changes in those areas in which I have an abiding interest. **"**

1992: Hillary explaining what kind of role she would play along with the perestroika pip-squeaks and glasnost eco-geeks that are sure to litter any potential Clinton administration.[16]

"Now we can talk about reality, and I would like to talk about reality sometime, authentic reality, inauthentic reality, and what we have to do to accept what we see. "

1969: Hillary demonstrating that life is often better represented by a dime-store novel than by a *missa solemnis.*[17]

## The Caveman Logic of Totalitarianism

" Collective action is needed on the community, state, and federal level to wrest from machines and those who profit from their use the extraordinary power they hold over us all. "

1978: Hillary articulating the anti-technology need to discover goats to scape in a brave attempt to usher in the benevolent reign of sundry bottom-rung bureaucrats and jacobin pink-squeaks.[18]

" Many of the modern conflicts between parents and children arise because of the invention of adolescence. Children in the Middle Ages became adults at the age of seven. . . . The concept of childhood was gradually expanded until children became more and more dependent on their parents and parents became less and less dependent on their children for economic support and sustenance. During the nineteenth century in this country, the idea of compulsory education provided an opportunity for children to be trained, and took them out of an increasingly smaller work force, so that they would not compete with adults. Child labor laws continued this trend and so did the imposition of age requirements for school attendance. . . . Because children now remain in the family for longer periods, during which they are still dependent but becoming more and more adult, the opportunities for intrafamily disputes have increased dramatically. **99**

1982: Hillary highlighting her Arimethean impulse to bury disparaged truth.[19]

" **A**merican women don't need lectures from Washington about values. . . . We don't need to hear about an idealized world that was never as righteous or carefree as some would like to think. "

1992: Hillary lecturing people about the ills of lecturing people—thus proving that even after weeks of a tortured national debate, she still didn't get it.[20]

## The Paternal State

> " I prefer that intervention into an ongoing family be limited to decisions that could have long-term and possible irreparable effects if they are not resolved. "

1979: Hillary translating "children's rights" into "government's rights" whenever and wherever the fuzzy-minded bureau-slugs see fit—or whenever and wherever the fancy grabs the paunchy redskis inside the Beltway.[21]

" The New World Foundation has sought to use its resources to strengthen the bridge— between the system and the neediest and least represented —and to encourage other foundations to focus on the fragility of activist and advocacy efforts on behalf of the poor in general and people of color in particular.

In this effort we have made mostly general support grants, rather than special project grants, so as to provide core support to organizers and advocates. **99**

1988: Hillary explaining why foundation grants should be given to the various radical and insurgent dialectical immaterialists—with no strings attached.[22]

" We need to be against brain-dead politics wherever we find it. "

1992: Hillary proving once again that hypocrisy is the tribute that error renders to truth, and inconsistency is the tribute that iniquity pays to integrity.[23]

**"I** sound like a candidate's wife . . . I have worked very hard to redefine the role I've inherited. **"**

1992: Hillary explaining how and why she has worked to change her controversial and bombastic image for the sake of the presidential race.[24]

❝ I want to be a voice for America's children . . . advocating . . . the immediate abolition of the legal status of minority and the reversal of the legal presumption of the incompetence of minors in favor of a presumption of competence; the extension to children of all procedural rights guaranteed to adults; the rejection of the legal presumption of the identity of interests between parents and their children, and permission for competent children to assert those independent interests in the courts. 〝〞

1974: Hillary arguing for the right of children to sue or even divorce their parents—and thus wandering into other people's dreams, never to find her way back.[25]

**❝I**ronically, reaction against state intervention in cases of nonphysical abuse is consistent with consensus romanticism about the family. ❞

1973: Hillary explaining why the politically-correct quota-facists, whining hobo-holdovers, and institutional purse-snatchers ought to be able to redefine the family for the rest of us poor unenlightened slobs.[26]

## The Magic of Logogogery and Logocide

" Words . . . are necessary . . . even in this multimedia age for attempting to come to grasp with some of the inarticulate, maybe even inarticulable things that we're feeling. "

1969: Hillary repeating the cant of sensitivity psychobabble—a talent she apparently picked up from the hipper-than-thou rumpled tweed crowd at Wellesley College.[27]

" The foundation has recognized the dilemma presented to public policy as federal support is withdrawn from social programs and social advocacy at the same time as the need for such programs grows more acute. As a result, philanthropy has had to serve as a bridge from the system to the neediest and the least represented. "

1988: Hillary rationalizing the need to direct huge sums of foundation charity dollars to anti-government fringe associations, counter-culture activist groups, and communist front organizations.[28]

" Certain myths . . . serve only to inhibit the development of a realistic family policy in this country: the myth of the housewife whose life centers only on her home and . . . the myth, or perhaps more accurately, the prejudice, that each family should be self-sufficient. "

1978: Hillary arguing for a new notion of "children's rights" in this happy milieu where all the rules have been violated and all the definitions have been vandalized.[29]

**"I** 'm not interested in attending a lot of funerals around the world. I want maneuverability. . . . I want to get deeply involved in solving problems. **"**

1992: Hillary dispelling any notion that she would stoop to mere symbolic gestures as a First Lady droid.[30]

## Flowers Power

# " This is the daughter of Willie Horton. "

1992: Hillary attempting to blame the persistent rumors of her husband's marital affair with Gennifer Flowers on campaign dirty-tricks—despite the fact that rumors of this and other dalliances had been floating around Arkansas for years.[31]

“ There is an absence of fair, workable, and realistic standards for limiting parental discretion and guiding state intervention. ”

1973: Hillary calling for greater prerogative on the part of the bureaucratic social service Goo-Goo Clusters to regulate all animate and most inanimate life forms within the known universe.[32]

" **W**e need to forge a new consensus about our political direction . . . that doesn't jerk us to the right, jerk us to the left, prey on our emotions, engender paranoia and insecurity . . . but instead moves us forward together. "

1992: Hillary deftly marshalling emotion, paranoia, and insecurity to rail against emotion, paranoia, and insecurity—all in the name of non-dogmatic dogmatism.[33]

" If the law were to abolish the status of minority and to reverse its assumption of children's incompetency, the result would be an implicit presumption that children, like other persons, are capable of exercising rights and assuming responsibilities until it is proven otherwise.

Empirical differences among children would then serve as the grounds for making exceptions to this presumption and for justifying rational state restrictions. **"**

1973: Hillary speaking in ecstatic tongues—in the practically uninterpretable language of American lawyerese—to call for more discretionary power for welfare apparatchinks and all the other collectivist no-goodniks.[34]

## How About a Yippie?

> " **I** 'm too old to be
> a yuppie. "

1992: Hillary rejecting the media's rather unaffected
baby-boom moniker for her.[35]

## Vigilante Battle Axe

# " I would crucify her. "

1992: Hillary describing what she would do to hapless Gennifer Flowers if she ever had the chance to assume the powers and prerogatives of the Sheriff of Nottingham—at least she doesn't intend to cut her heart out with a spoon.[36]

" A common complaint about the exercise of discretion in neglect cases is that alien values, usually middle class, are used to judge a family's child-rearing practices. One way to answer that complaint is to entrust the discretion necessary for evaluating a child's needs to persons representing the milieu in which a family lives. "

1973: Hillary assuring skeptics that the social service rabble assigned to take children away from their parents should not be tainted with certain ethnocentristic morals—God forbid that middle class values should compromise the politburo efficiency of those government poltroons.[37]

## Who Else Would She Be?

“ **I** hope I’m going to be myself. ”

1992: Hillary describing how she’ll act once she and her hubby are safely ensconced in that really cool, big house on Pennsylvania Avenue.[38]

"We believe that a worthwhile life is defined by a kind of spiritual journey and a sense of obligation that is, for us, not burdensome. It's liberating, it's wonderful, and it's fun."

1992: Hillary describing her New Age real-good, feel-good ethical beliefs.[39]

## Your Mama Don't Dance,
## and Your Daddy Don't Rock and Roll

" **C**hildren should have a right to decide their future if they are competent. "

1979: Hillary summing up her nutty "family values" plank in a nutshell.[40]

" **M**odern communications haven't figured out yet how to present complex reality. Television flattens experience. It flattens people. It is a two-dimensional experience, not three. "

1992: Hillary explaining the grand paradox of why it is reprehensible to pick on Murphy Brown if you are a conservative while it is imperative to pick on Murphy Brown if you are a liberal.[41]

## Attention, K-Mart Shoppers

“ **I**f you vote for my husband, you get me; it's a two-for-one, blue plate special. ”

1992: Hillary explaining this year's political equivalent of the K-Mart blue-light-special.[42]

" **I** have a hard time
projecting what will
happen after this election. "

1992: Hillary discussing the future with one ravenous
and one Lenten eye—with both the White House and
the dog house in view.[43]

> " I t was a personal
> decision, but it was
> prompted by political
> considerations. "

1992: Hillary offering an explanation for her conde-
scension in finally taking her husband's last name
seven years after their marriage—apparently, Slick's
demographic surveys and focus groups pulled more
weight than any love-honor-and-obey troth.[44]

**" T** he fear that many people have about . . . a law of children's rights arises from their concern about increasing government control over such intra-family disputes. **"**

1979: Hillary pooh-poohing the notion that yielding familial compelling interests to the government might be an undesirable trend—the dumb certainties of experience do count for something.[45]

" **T**he real scandal is who dug up all those old pictures of me. "

1992: Hillary humorously responding to the exposure that the unending string of scandals that dogged the Clinton primary campaign brought—the press published several unflattering photos of her before handlers had remade her dowdy feminazi image.[46]

" Words have a funny
way of trapping
our minds on the
way to our tongues. "

1969: Hillary offering proof positive that the callouses
on her conscience give her a delirious freedom to
abandon the fussy philistine claims of logic as well
as its monotonous sequentiality.[47]

## Part Three

# HOPE

*Answer a fool according to his folly, lest he be wise in his own eyes. He who sends a message by the hand of a fool cuts off his own feet and drinks violence. Like the legs of the lame that hang limp is a proverb in the mouth of fools.*

*Proverbs 26:5–7*

Ghost-writing speech wiz Peggy Noonan said she'd been picking up "great speech ions" for days before the Democratic National Convention.[1] But apparently the ions lied. Bill Clinton's acceptance oratory was a bonafide clunker.

The speech was supposed to "reposition" Clinton, to "reintroduce him to the electorate," and to "revive his standing as the Post-Perot alternative to politics-as-usual." It was supposed to resonate with "middle America's blue-collar and suburban voters." It was supposed to demonstrate genuine "leadership and confidence." But it did none of those things.

Instead, the speech was a lurid scatological mumbo-jumbo of whining Twelve-Step recovery platitudes, yammering zen-political slogans, touchy-feely existential introspection, and gushy prime-time applause-lines—all as hollow as they were insipid. It was strident in its Hare Krishna disregard for substantive analysis or political reality. It was disjointed, dispiriting, and discumboomerated. It was an Orwellian exposition of some sort of New Age pop-aesthetic dogma. In short, Clinton squandered his moment of glory—regardless of what blips and surges the polls may indicate—by assuming that Republicans have dominated seven of the last ten presidential elections "with lines, not ideas."[2]

In other words, his speech was *hillarious*—rooted in the shallow and silly worldview of his wife and her radical cohorts.

Not that Clinton could have rooted the speech in anything else. He could ill afford to attempt to root it in the humus of his record as a can-do politician with workable policy proposals and a successful public policy track-record, for instance. After four terms in the Governor's mansion, Arkansas remains an economic and educational disaster—only three states have a higher rate of poverty, a lower per capita income, and fewer people on the federal welfare dole.[3] He has overseen the decline of the state's public school system—now ranking among the worst in the nation—as well as both its agricultural and industrial bases.[4] He has raised taxes 128 times, and yet he still has found balancing the budget a nearly impossible task.[5]

Thus, Clinton and his wife—hungry with presidential ambition—were stuck with the threadbare fabric of a failed ideology, with the crazy-quilt baggage of a failed coalition, and the tired rhetoric of a failed worldview. And all that in the name of a "New Covenant" that would supposedly protect "the rights of the people" and ensure "liberty and justice for all."[6]

## War of the Worlds

On October 27, 1787, Alexander Hamilton predicted that a "dangerous ambition" would one day tyrannize the gangling young American Republic, all the while lurking "behind the specious mask of zeal for the *rights* of the people."[7]

It could almost be said that Hamilton had the Democratic *hillarious* "New Covenant" in mind when he wrote that—were it not for the difficulty of chronology. Certainly, its ideas legitimately fall under the purview of his warning. The "New Covenant" is, in fact, rather old. And, it has already exercised its "dangerous ambition" in other forms and incarnations, all across our land in legislatures, courtrooms, bureaucracies, classrooms, social service agencies, and communities—wreaking havoc on our families, our neighborhoods, our schools, our businesses, and our system of justice. And it has done this, all the while lurking behind the "specious mask" that Hamilton described so long ago. It has done this, all the while simultaneously championing "the *rights* of the people."

What this political and covenantal conception has done, though—as awful and tyrannical as it has *been*—is not nearly as disconcerting as what it actually *is*. Its actions and activities are merely symptoms of a deeper, darker cancer. They are merely the outward expressions of its "dangerous ambition."

That "ambition" is actually a worldview.

The word *worldview* is a poor English attempt at translating the German *weltanschauung*. It literally means a philosophical orientation, a life perspective, or a life integrator.

You have a worldview. I have a worldview. Everyone does.

Our worldview is simply the way we look at things. It is our perspective of reality. It is the means by which we interpret the situations and circumstances around us. It is what enables us to integrate all the different aspects of our life, faith, and experience. Alvin Toffler, in his landmark book *Future Shock,* said, "Every person carries in his head a mental model of the world, a subjective representation of external reality."[8] This mental model is, he says, like a giant filing cabinet. It contains a slot for every item of information coming to us. It organizes our knowledge and gives us a grid from which to think. Our mind is not as Locke or Voltaire would have us suppose: a *tabula rasa*, blank and impartial. Our viewpoint is not open and objective. "When we think," says economic philosopher E. F. Schumacher, "we can only do so because our mind is already filled with all sorts of ideas with which to think."[9] These more or less fixed ideas make up our mental model of the world, our frame of reference, our presuppositions—or, in other words, our worldview.

James Sire tells us:

> A worldview is a map of reality; and like any map, it may fit what is really there, or it may be grossly misleading. The map is not the world itself, of course, only an image of it, more or less accurate in some places, distorted in others. Still, all of us carry around such a map in our mental makeup and we act upon it. All of our thinking presupposes it. Most of our experience fits into it.[10]

Throughout the history of mankind, there have been any number of worldviews espoused by ardent and articulate partisans. But, there is one particular worldview that has become only too familiar to us—actually dominating our cultural apparatus—in these modern times. That worldview, and the adherents that extol its virtues, have been brilliantly described by the twentieth century's foremost historian, Paul Johnson:

> With the decline of clerical power in the eighteenth century, a new kind of mentor emerged to fill the vacuum and capture the ear of society. The secular intellectual might be deist, skeptic, or atheist. But he was just as ready as any pontiff or presbyter to tell mankind how

to conduct its affairs. He proclaimed from the start, a special devotion to the interests of humanity and an evangelical duty to advance them by his teaching. He brought to this self-appointed task a far more radical approach than his clerical predecessors. He felt himself bound by no corpus of revealed religion. The collective wisdom of the past, the legacy of tradition, the prescriptive codes of ancestral experience existed to be selectively followed or wholly rejected entirely as his own good sense might decide. For the first time in human history, and with growing confidence and audacity, men arose to assert that they could diagnose the ills of society and cure them with their own unaided intellects: more, that they could devise formulae whereby not merely the structure of society but the fundamental habits of human beings could be transformed for the better. Unlike their sacerdotal predecessors, they were not servants and interpreters of the gods but substitutes. Their hero was Prometheus, who stole the celestial fire and brought it to earth.[11]

The worldview that Johnson is describing is what has recently come to be called *secular humanism*. It is the worldview that the "dangerous ambition" of the Clinton campaign epitomizes and espouses.

According to Francis Schaeffer, secular humanism is "the placing of man at the center of all things and making him the measure of all things."[12] According to Aleksandr Solzhenitsyn, it is "the proclaimed and practiced autonomy of man from any higher force above him."[13] In the humanistic system, there is no ultimate standard of right or wrong. There are no clear-cut ethical paradigms. Morality is relative. Problem solving is entirely subjective. Paradoxically then, the only absolute is that there are no absolutes.

In direct contradistinction to humanism—and serving as its chief adversary—is what the Founding Fathers of this great experiment in liberty first called the "American Covenant." According to this system, there are indeed standards, paradigms, and absolutes. They are unwavering ethical standards rooted in the traditions, lessons, and verities of Western Christendom.

All those who have gone on before us laying the foundations of freedom that we now enjoy—forefathers, fathers, patriarchs, and prophets—have had this perspective as the foundation and frame of their worldview.

The radical activists and social reformers in Hillary and Bill's revitalized Democratic "New Covenant" alliance certainly cannot be faulted for their concern for the rights of people—to the extent that they really are concerned about those rights. Where they have gone wrong—and ultimately what makes their "ambition" so "dangerous"—is in taking matters into their own hands. It is in stealing the "celestial fire." It is in canonizing their own new and novel notions—of law, morality, social relations, and whatever else. Instead of adhering to the tried and true patterns of freedom—walking along the well trod path of the pioneers of liberty—they have "each one turned to his own way,"[14] and done "what is right in his own eyes."[15]

That is a far cry from the worldview that gave rise to the great flowering of culture and freedom that Americans have enjoyed over the past two hundred years.

The tag-team Clintons advocate change. They are adherents of a new worldview and a new covenant. They have new ideas. But, they are the same *old* new ideas—and the same *old* new worldview and covenant—that the enemies of this civilization have always marshalled against freedom and liberty.

## Two Revolutions

A change in worldview necessarily means a change in the nature of society. That anthropological, sociological, and theological fact was borne out in a very vivid fashion during the late eighteenth century during the tumultuous aftermath of the American and French Revolutions.

That revolutionary era ushered in an ethos of convulsing paradox and enrapturing cataclysm that was captured in the opening scene of *A Tale of Two Cities,* the riveting novel by Charles Dickens:

> It was the best of times, it was the worst of times, it was the age of wisdom, it was the age of foolishness, it was the epoch of belief, it was the epoch of incredulity, it was the season of Light, it was the season of Darkness, it was the spring of hope, it was the winter of despair, we had everything before us, we had nothing before us, we were all going directly to Heaven, we were all going direct the other way.[16]

The passage concludes saying:

> In short, the period was so far like the present period, that some of its noisiest authorities insisted on its being received, for good or for evil, in the superlative degree of comparison only.[17]

The dichotomous nature of the era that Dickens first describes and then applies, was surely the result of the dichotomous relationship of its two great events: the American Revolution of 1776 and the French Revolution of 1789.

Two more widely polarized yet interdependent events cannot possibly be dredged from the tattered annals of Western Civilization. Though, by all appearances, they were like *dideros* and *videros*—practically identical in seed, root, sprig, blossom, and fruit—they were, in fact, as different as *chalmedia* and *tralmedia*—entirely unrelated genuses.[18] Indeed, as Stephen Higginson has asserted, the two revolutions actually "drew a red-hot ploughshare through history."[19]

According to the prominent American historian Garry Wills:

> There were two great revolutions against European monarchs in the late eighteenth century. In the first, the French nation helped Americans achieve their independence from George III. Without that help, our revolution could not have succeeded. Yet when the French rebelled against Louis XVI, Americans at first merely hailed their action, then hesitated over it, and finally recoiled from it.[20]

Why was that? Why did the Founding Fathers of the newly independent American republic reject their brothers-in-arms from across the Atlantic? Why did they not rally to the Jacobin cry of "Liberty, Equality, and Fraternity"? Why did they not rush to the aid of the embattled masses of France struggling to be free of a monarchial tyrant?

The answer is simple: worldview. The American leaders recognized that the worldview of the French Jacobins was rooted in the humanistic covenant and was thus entirely incompatible with their own—that it was in fact, detrimental to their own.

The American revolution was a covenantal response to what was perceived to be a graceless trouncing of the rule of law. It gave rise to an extraordinary and unparalleled reign of freedom, peace, and prosperity. It was a *conservative* movement in the sense of *returning* the estate of the nation to the *old* virtues of Christendom.[21] The former royal colonists understood the term *revolution* in the Copernican sense of *coming full circle, to revolve,* or *to return to an original state.* Thus, they conducted themselves with the utmost in decorum and ethics.

The French Revolution, on the other hand, was a covenantally deliberate affront to Western traditions. It gave rise to a horrifying reign of anarchy and terror that cost the lives of tens of thousands of innocent citizens and burned itself out in brazen licentiousness and concupiscence. It was a *liberal* movement in the sense of *dispatching* the estate of the nation from the *old* virtues of Christendom while ushering the *new* amoralities of the Enlightenment.[22] The former royal subjects understood the term *revolution* in the Rousseauian sense of *starting anew, to revolt,* or *to overthrow a former state.* Thus, they conducted themselves with the height of perversion and violence.

Rhetorically and theoretically, both revolutions made much over the ideals of liberty, freedom, and justice. But, whereas the American effort had scattered seeds of faithfulness, forthrightness, fealty, and fulfillment to the four corners of the earth, the French effort had sown seeds of doubt, dissension, discord, and devastation to the four winds. The American revolution was a "lofty aspiration" exercised. The French revolution was a "dangerous ambition" exorcised.

It was with this understanding as a backdrop that Alexander Hamilton decried the French disruptions in a letter to his friend, the Marquis de Lafayette, saying:

> When I contemplate the horrid and systematic massacres of the Jacobins; when I observe that a Marat and a Robespierre, the notorious promoters of those bloody scenes, sit triumphantly in the convention and take a conspicuous part in its measures, that an attempt to bring the assassins to justice has been obliged to be abandoned; when I see an unfortunate prince, whose reign was a continued demonstration of the goodness and benevolence of his heart, his attachment to the people of whom he was the monarch, who though educated in the lap of despotism, had given repeated proofs that *he was not the enemy of liberty*, brought precipitately and ignominiously to the block without any substantial proof of guilt as yet disclosed—without even

an authentic exhibition of motives in decent regard to the opinions of mankind; *when I find the doctrines of Atheism openly advanced in the convention and heard with loud applause;* when I see the sword of *fanaticism* extended to force a political creed upon citizens who were invited to submit to the arms of France as the harbingers of liberty; when I behold *the hand of rapacity* outstretched to prostrate and ravish the monuments of religious worship erected by those citizens and their ancestors; when I perceive passion, tumult, and violence usurping those seats where reason and cool deliberation ought to prevail, I acknowledge that I am glad to believe *there is no real resemblance between what was the cause of America and what is the cause of France; that the difference is no less great than the difference between liberty and licentiousness.* I regret whatever has the tendency to compound them, and I feel anxious as an American, that the ebullitions of inconsiderate men among us may not tend to involve our reputation in the issue.[23]

Hamilton understood that the worldview of the French revolutionaries would inevitably lead them—and all those around them—into a quagmire of death and destruction regardless of their slogans or intentions. He knew that true and lasting liberty is simply not possible apart from the gracious environs of the traditional worldview of the West. And any attempt to so achieve it is doomed. It is a "dangerous ambition." In fact, he ominously predicted that:

> After wading through seas of blood, France may find herself at length the slave of some victorious Sulla or Marius or Caesar.[24]

Within six years of that prophesy, Napoleon had indeed usurped the authority of the republican leadership—or what was left of it after more than a decade of utter chaos. France was then plunged into the darkest chapter in its long history, and Europe began its long and tortured struggle with one tyrant after another.

Hamilton was no seer. He simply comprehended the impact and end result of the revolution's presuppositions. He was perceptive enough to look past its first appearances to consider its root. He knew that cosmetic adjustments in France's policies or programs would not make any substantial difference in the nation's ultimate destiny. He recognized that for life, liberty, and the pursuit of happiness to be restored to France, the humanistic worldview would have to be uprooted and replaced. More importantly, though, he realized that in order for America to maintain its own liberty, the "dangerous ambition" of humanism had to be kept out of our social institutions.

That is enough motivation, in and of itself, to protect the "American Covenant" from the onslaughts of Hillary and Bill's "New Covenant."

What ails the Democratic Party is fatal, but not serious. It is *hillarious*—and that is no laughing matter. And yet, there is hope still. Despite this revolutionary clamor, the old covenant has yet to be supplanted by the new. For as G. K. Chesterton has asserted:

> Weak things must boast of being new, like so many German philosophies. But strong things can boast of being old. Strong things can boast of being moribund.[25]

In the end, the silly and superfluous must succumb to the substantial. Amen.

# NOTES

## Apologia

1. Marvin Burl Matthews, *Laughter and Medicine*, (London: Carlton and Lambert, 1946), p. 67.

## Part One: Hype

1. *C-Span*, July 14, 1992.
2. *C-Span*, July 15, 1992.
3. *Wall Street Journal*, January 31, 1992.
4. *Newsweek*, March 30, 1992.
5. *New York Times*, May 18, 1992.
6. *Vanity Fair*, June 1992.
7. Ibid.
8. *National Review*, July 20, 1992.
9. Ibid.
10. Ibid.
11. Ibid.
12. *American Spectator*, August 1992.
13. *Wall Street Journal*, March 13, 1992.
14. Ibid.
15. *National Review*, July 20, 1992.
16. *Human Events*, April 25, 1992.
17. *National Review*, July 20, 1992.
18. Ibid.
19. *American Spectator*, August 1992.
20. *National Review*, July 20, 1992.
21. *American Spectator*, August 1992.

## Part Two: Hyperbole

1. *New York Times*, March 17, 1992.

2. *American Spectator*, August 1992.

3. Ibid.

4. Ibid.

5. *60 Minutes*, January 26, 1992.

6. *Yale Law Journal*, vol. 86: 1522, 1977.

7. *American Spectator*, August 1992.

8. *Newsweek*, March 30, 1992.

9. *Washington Times*, May 30, 1992.

10. *CBS This Morning*, April 3, 1992.

11. *People*, July 20, 1992.

12. Ibid.

13. *American Spectator*, August 1992.

14. Ibid.

15. *Newsweek*, March 30, 1992.

16. Ibid.

17. *American Spectator*, August 1992.

18. *Public Welfare*, Winter 1978.

19. *American Spectator*, August 1992.

20. *Washington Times*, May 30, 1992.

21. *American Spectator*, August 1992.

22. Ibid.

23. *Vanity Fair*, June 1992.

24. *Wall Street Journal*, January 31, 1992.

25. *Harvard Educational Review*, 1974.

26. *Harvard Educational Review*, November 1973.

27. *American Spectator*, August 1992.

28. Ibid.

29. *Public Welfare*, Winter 1978.

30. *Vanity Fair*, June 1992.

31. *Vanity Fair*, June 1992.

32. *Harvard Educational Review*, November 1973.

33. *Vanity Fair*, June 1992.

34. *Harvard Educational Review*, November 1973.

35. *New York Times*, May 18, 1992.

36. *Vanity Fair*, June 1992.

37. *Harvard Educational Review*, November 1973.

38. *New York Times*, May 18, 1992.

39. *People*, July 20, 1992.

40. *American Spectator*, August 1992.

41. *People*, July 20, 1992.

42. *CBS This Morning*, April 3, 1992.

43. *Washington Times*, May 6, 1992.

44. *ABC PrimeTime*, January 30, 1992.

45. *American Spectator*, August 1992.

46. *Washington Times*, May 6, 1992.

47. *American Spectator*, August 1992.

## Part Three: Hope

1. *Newsweek*, July 27, 1992.

2. Ibid.

3. *National Review*, July 20, 1992.

4. *Washington Times*, July 14, 1992.

5. *U.S. News and World Report*, July 20, 1992.

6. *New York Times*, July 17, 1992.

7. *Conservative Digest*, December. 1988.

8. Alvin Toffler, *Future Shock*, (New York: Bantam, 1971), p. 158.

9. E. F. Schumacher, *Small Is Beautiful*, (New York: Harper and Row, 1975), p. 52.

10. James Sire, *How to Read Slowly*, (Wheaton, IL: Harold Shaw Publishers, 1978, 1989), pp. 14–15.

11. Paul Johnson, *Intellectuals*, (New York: Harper and Row, 1989), pp. 1–2.

12. Francis A. Schaeffer, *A Christian Manifesto*, (Westchester, IL: Crossway Books, 1981), p. 24.

13. Aleksandr I. Solzhenitsyn, *A World Split Apart*, (New York: Harper and Row, 1978), pp. 47–49.

14. Isaiah 53:6.

15. Judges 2:25.

16. Charles Dickens, *A Tale of Two Cities*, (London: Penguin Classics, 1859, 1970), p. 35.

17. Ibid.

18. Umberto Eco, *The Open Work* (Cambridge, MA: Harvard University Press, 1988).

19. *American Heritage*, August, 1989.

20. Ibid.

21. See, Tim LaHaye, *Faith of Our Founding Fathers*, (Brentwood, TN: Wolgemuth and Hyatt, Publishers, 1987); Marshall Foster and Mary Elaine Swanson, *The American Covenant*, (Medford, OR: The Mayflower Institute, 1983); and, Franklin P. Cole, *They Preached Liberty*, (Indianapolis, IN: Liberty Press, 1981).

22. See, Francois Furet and Denis Richet, *The French Revolution*, (New York: Macmillan, 1970); James H. Billington, *Fire in the Minds of Men*, (New York: Basic Books, 1980); John Adams, *Discourses on Davila*, (Boston: American Primary Texts, 1790, 1936); Edmund Burke, *Reflections on the Revolution in France*, (New York: Paperbound Classics, 1792, 1958); and, Alexander Hamilton, *The Cause of France*, (New York: E. M. Farber and Sons, 1793, 1899).

23. Henry Cabot Lodge, *Alexander Hamilton*, (New York: Charles Scribner's Sons, 1899, 1922), pp. 253–254.

24. *The World and I*, July 1989.

25. Marvin Burl Matthews, *Laughter and Medicine*, (London: Carlton and Lambert, 1946), p. 67.

# AUTHOR

G EORGE GRANT is a popular speaker and best-selling author. He has written more than a dozen books including *Perot: The Populist Appeal of Strong-Man Politics* and *The Last Crusader: The Untold Story of Christopher Columbus*. Grant has also written a survey of the on-going crisis in the Middle East, an exposé of the American Civil Liberties Union, and an award-winning critique of Planned Parenthood. He is the Executive Director of **Legacy Communications,** a research and educational resource organization. His academic studies in political science were conducted at the University of Houston. He lives with his wife and children in middle Tennessee where he is currently at work on several new writing projects including a series of historical and biographical profiles.

For information about newsletters or speaking schedules of Mr. Grant, please contact:

**ADROIT PRESS**
P.O. Box 680365
Franklin, TN 37068

## Credits

*Front cover photograph:*   Allan Tannenbaum / Sygma

*Photographs on pages 33, 37, 41, 53, 57, 65, 69, 71, 75:*   Ira Wyman / Sygma

*Photographs on pages 27, 73:*   Allan Tannenbaum / Sygma

*Photograph on page 67:*   Jeffrey Markowitz / Sygma

*Photograph on page 49:*   Paul Meridet / Sygma

*Photographs on pages 35, 77:*   Sygma

*Photograph on page 29:*   Malcolme Clarke / AP

*Photograph on page 51:*   Doug Mills / AP

*Photograph on page 43:*   Jim Sulley / AP

*Photograph on page 61:*   Charles Rex Arbogest / AP

*Cover Design:*   Koechel-Peterson
Minneapolis, Minnesota

*Typography:*   MountainView / Editing & Book Design
Franklin, Tennessee